Musical
Love
Theory

Introduction: An Author's Message

"An Author's Message"

(A message from me to my readers)

Dark clouds form a forecasting shadow,
Complicated to most but transparent to me.
Raindrops and tears are one in the same,
What is joy without first feeling pain?
Reality and fantasy become equal partners,
As both leave my mind and connect with my heart.
From my heart both areas meet on these pages,
Therefore creating stanzas to be read throughout the ages.
Let these words speak when my mouth can't form words,
Allow them to continue to breathe long after my demise.
For even in death I shall live 4ever,
In one beautiful realm, that is in the eyes and hearts of my readers.

Chapter I: Modern Day Philosophy

“Modern Day Philosophy”

A confused mind also has a fragile heart,
Twisted thoughts also have logical meanings.
Pain is pain and love is blind,
A blind person falls deep in love without a shield.
Issues affect that person so now there’s pain,
Is it safe to say that pain is love?
Or is it safe to say that love is misery?
Misery needs company and loves needs a cause.
Questions need answers and hopes turn to dreams,
Dreams turn to achievements only if there’s a strong belief.
So who or what is it you believe in?
What drives you or are you just being lead blinded?
Do you play the game or are you being played?
Do you play to win or do you play not to lose?
Sometimes when you win, you actually lose.
And when you lose, you actually win,
If you should tie, you might actually win or lose.
And if you win or lose, you might actually tie.
What confuses you makes sense to me,
And if it doesn’t confuse you then we both understand.
If no one is in the woods and a tree falls down,
Is it safe to say there isn’t a sound made?
If someone is crying does it mean they’re upset?
If someone flashes a smile does it mean they’re not hurting?
Death is often called the Afterlife,
The Afterlife is called the Other-side.
So what is on the Other-side, which comes Afterlife?
And if death is on the Other-side, then where are we now?
Are we on the Other-side of the other side or simply on another side?
Questions come from ideas and answers need reasons,
I search 2 find answers because my dreams need detail.

"A Bully Named **FEAR**"

Fear…what does it mean 2 you? What is it that really scares you? One must face his or her fear and destroy it before it destroys you! Fear is nothing more than a simple emotion. We can all go back 2 our childhoods and recall bullies. What is it that made a bully "invincible"? How could one person or a group of individuals strike fear into another person or persons? The answer 2 that question is quite simple. The reason why bullies seemed so invincible had nothing 2 do with their size. Small individuals struck fear into larger individuals and vice versa. The "strength in numbers" theory isn't a major issue either. The reason bullies controlled so many people is due 2 the lack of **FEAR** that was used 2 inject **FEAR**. A bully had the mind frame of not being scared of anything. They had no **FEAR** when it came 2 taking milk and lunch money. Most of their crew members **FEARED** the leader of the crew as well. As long as they had the **FEAR** factor on their side, they had no reason 2 **FEAR** anything. Once that day came where you felt like the bullies couldn't scare you, you stood up 4 yourself. You either won or took a loss but either way you stood up 4 yourself. That's all **FEAR** really is, a big or small bully with friends. Its friends are the reasons that your mind retains which keeps you afraid. All we as people have 2 do is stand up! Once we battle that **FEAR**, no matter how bruised we may be, at least we faced the **FEAR**. Without inner strength, **FEAR** will simply consume us. You can either face your **FEARS** or 4ever run and be a victim. The choice is yours.

"Just how it is"

To take away doesn't always mean you're losing,
To have something doesn't always mean you've gained,
Just because you learn doesn't mean you're smart,
When love is gone you still have your heart,
You can't trust everyone you meet,
That statement is a simple fact.
What you see isn't always what you get,
Some things are the way they are.

“True Statements”

He who hesitates at war is lost,
He who doesn’t speak has nothing to say,
Those who “act” merely lie to themselves,
Those who try too hard don’t always achieve,
Love won’t love you back,
You have to love yourself before loving anyone else.
Failure is the stepping-stone to success,
Cowards often die a thousand deaths.

“Words To Grown On”

He who believes not in himself,
Believes in everything else that isn’t true.
The true character of a person shouldn’t be judged by their actions,
But solely on how they bounce back from adversity.
All of life’s lessons can’t be taught at a university,
Some things are merely common sense.
Trust and believe, seek and you shall find,
The light at the very end of the tunnel,
Instead of living life outside or inside of the box,
Try living as if there is no box at all.

"Something to Think About"

To live is to learn to learn is to search,
To search is to find to find is to treasure,
Treasure what's learned and teach it to others,
Honestly we all need each other.
Be true to yourself b4 you trust others,
How can you love the next person if you don't love yourself?

To have is to gain to gain is to hold,
To hold is to keep until the end of time.
Time isn't what you think and the second you blink,
That particular time is gone 4ever.
Be true to yourself b4 you trust others,
How can you trust anyone if you don't know yourself?

"Asking Questions"

The only question I have is simply why?
Why did my friends and family have to suddenly die?
How come when people die rain falls from the sky?
How come authority figures like the President tell lies?
Why do we believe what we see on TV?
Why am I looked at funny when my people see me?
Why do I tell the youth not to follow our lead?
Why am I in such a rush to plant a seed?
Why am I hating life yet scared to die?
Though it's been years why are my people afraid to fly?
Why did my ex do me wrong but won't admit it?
And if I knew the truth why did I remain committed?
Why do I hate my job but continue to go?
Why do I see the right path but just won't go?
How come I see my death in some of my dreams?
How come my songs and poetry are totally different?
Is there a reason why I cry?
I just don't know,
And if the answers are out there when will they show?

"Receiving Answers"

Every question has an answer.
Everyone must die no one is immortal.
Raindrops fall when people die to signify God's happiness for bringing his children home.
Everyone lies it's just that authority figures have good lawyers to beat the case.
Television paints an image so life like we can't help but believe it.
People tend to judge based upon what they see.
We tell the youth not to make our same mistakes because we've been where they are.
I'm not rushing to have a seed; it's just that I something/someone here to continue my legacy that way I'll live 4ever.
Life ain't always easy but death could be worse.
People are afraid to fly because the nightmare of September 11th still lingers on.
Some people just can't commit so she (my ex) decided that lying was a good option.
Ultimately she was just a scared girl.
When –n- love you see what you want to see. I saw the answers but chose not to read them.
No one really enjoys his or her job. I'm just addicted to getting money so that's why I'm there.
Sometime we know what to do but don't know what to do; life is a lesson.
We all have images of death. I just see mine quite vividly.
There are two sides of me; each side is displayed through my different talents.
I cry 4 many reasons.
All of my questions have just been answered.

"Commitment"

When it comes to commitment why do we run from it?
We all say we need it but what do we want from it?
Just when you think you've found the one you can commit to,
They up and find a way to show their true colors.
How can you be faithful when someone's cheating on you?
Once you c the truth it hurts like a bad tooth.
Most of the time we commit to what we c,
But what we c ain't always what we get.
When is the right time or who is the right one?
Those are questions that hold many answers.
We all want to have our cake and eat it too,
Which means we want to commit and be able to cheat too.
In order to commit you can't run from it,
And b4 you can commit know what you want from it.

"Connections"

The things that are often written in multiple notebooks,
Are in a twisted way connected to the words I speak.
The statements that are often spoken,
Are strangely connected to the thoughts *they* think.
Who is really right, who is actually wrong?
What is the difference between right and wrong?
Everything in life happens with a balance,
That's because life is filled with a balance of imbalances.
Good doesn't exist without evil,
Evil doesn't exist with good,
Everything somehow is strangely connected,
Every ying must have a yang.
After the storm a rainbow appears,
Through the cloudy sky peaks a joyful sunray.
Angels belong to the Lord like demons reside with Satan,
But Satan was once one of God's angels.
All good things must come to an end,
Most painful situations create positive outcomes.
No matter the situation you can be sure of this,
Everything in life has a twisted yet logical connection.

"Learning"

I don't ask for much so what I get is just that,
No more, no less, but there's a lesson in that.
You get what you ask for and most times you find,
That the things you want most actually make you blind.
What does it mean when all you do is dream?
You visualize then realize things ain't the way they seem.
The grass ain't always green,
So on the other side ain't where I reside.
I play on the fence; drive in through the middle,
Of the fork in the road don't view this as a riddle.
It's not that hard but it's far from simple,
It is what it is so I strive 4 more.
I don't ask for much so what I get is just that,
No more, no less, but there's a lesson in that.

Chapter II: Not Just Poetry

"Words 4 My People"

We struggle 2 find our way,
And we stumble throughout our struggles,
We strive 4 equality,
But what we're lacking is unity,
We are the have-nots,
The ones who want peace,
If it comes down 2 it,
We will also bring war,
We are the falsely accused,
We are the battered and bruised,
We are often misunderstood,
We get frequently used,
But "they" brought us here,
2 become their slaves,
Now the tables have turned,
And some of "them" work 4 us,
Now they scream, "Go back 2 where you come from"
But like I said before it was "you" that brought us here,
Now they're made because the things they showed us,
Have been flipped around now we are our own bosses,
We own our own companies,
No longer take orders,
Now some of "you" get the donuts and fetch the water,
Baby-sit our sons and daughters,
Paint our fences,
Clean our homes,
Wash our clothes,
Answer our phones,
Take our messages,
Tell us jokes,
Makes us laugh,
How does it feel 2 have the tables turned?
Fair is fair, we keep the bridges standing but "you" want them burned,
We grabbed books, pens and pads and we learned,
The only way "you" kept us ignorant,
Was by keeping us blinded,
Now we can read and write,
And if our backs are against the wall,
Best believe we fight!
No matter what we face,
We must keep the Lord 1st,
In the face of adversity,
We will always unite.

"Based on a true story"

(After the car crash)

In the blink of an eye my life almost ended,
I watched my whole life flash right before my eyes.
Heavy eyelids led to one near fatal blink,
I saw trees and bushes and then I heard a loud crash.
The impact forced my head backwards,
Then out came the air bag,
I thank God I had on my seatbelt.
Everything turned black and when I opened my eyes,
The entire car was up in smoke.
The drivers side door was locked and I began to panic,
I heard a voice tell me to check the other door.
My heart was racing and the door seemed stuck,
So rolled down the window and I climbed out.
I hurried and ran away from the car,
Caring individuals soon came to my aid.
As I looked back at my car it seemed unreal,
The car was smashed up like it was a toy.
The only objects I grabbed were my coat and this very book,
Everyone at the seen looked at me strangely.
Based upon the damage they said I was lucky,
Just 5 days before my 22nd birthday I could've passed away.
Life has changed 4 me and I'm grateful 4 each new day.
How did I manage to escape with no scars?
It's quite obvious there must be a God.
Someone or something up above was with me this evening,
Life isn't as long as we expect it to be.
I'm lucky to be alive because I could be gone,
All I can do now is be thankful and carry on.

"Next In Line"

As I sit and observe her,
Many things cross my mind,
I noticed that all of her movements,
Are breathtaking and flawless.
Her eyes tell the story,
That her mouth can't speak,
She seems haunted by her past,
Which presently cripples her future.
If only I could talk with her,
There's so much to speak,
If only she'd look my way,
And let this journey begin.
But at this moment,
She is very busy with her work,
So I will simply sit here,
And watch from a distance.
Time flew away,
Like a leaf in the wind,
And before I knew it,
My time had come.
I didn't know what to say,
But I continued on,
In the blink of an eye,
We were face to face.
She opened her mouth,
And out came an angelic voice,
I'll never 4get her first words,
Which were "May I help you?"

“Lost Little Girl”
(After the News)

She used to be a little girl with big dreams and pretty eyes,
At any time her smile could outshine the sun.
If life was a game, I taught her the rules,
I told her focus on school and pay no mind to dudes.
I’m not ‘Pac(Tupac Shakur) but she always kept her eyes on me,
If I was wrong or right she would side with me.
As she grew she didn’t spend a lot of time with me,
I guess I never took the time to see,
That my baby girl grew and switched sides on me,
I was hurt when I learned she’d be lying to me.
Cool tempered and calm is what I was trying to be,
But the pain is hard to swallow.
I made her a path that she chose not to follow,
Where do I go from here?
How can a smile turn to tears?
It’s easy, all you have to do is cry.
The same face that I trusted has me questioned,
It’s a shame to see my baby girl is lost.
I hate to let her go and just leave her alone,
Maybe in time she’ll change and return home.

“I Had No Clue”

Why do you sit there all alone?
There’s so much out here for you to do.
If you need company I can hang with you,
She simply looked, smiled then walked away.

Why are you walking around all alone?
There are so many people walking around you.
If you need company I can hang with you,
She simply looked, smiled then kept on walking.

I had to stop her in hopes to see,
If I could hang with this lady but she kept walking,
Once I finally stopped her she talked with her hands,
The reason she never spoke was because she’s deaf.

"Murderville"(Part 1)

You want to know where I stay?
Ok, I'll tell you, hopefully you'll keep an open mind.
I live in Murderville, which is part of Suicide City,
Every time I take a trip, demons often ride with me.
My house is located on 1-8-7 lane,
Next to Homicide Drive and Drive-By Court.
In Murderville we have no place to place games,
Everyday chains get snatched and brains are displayed.
Crack-heads roam like cell phones looking 4 a fix,
Street walkers pace the block looking 4 new tricks.
As 4 me, I just chill and observe the sights,
I often dance with the devil in the pale moonlight.
Yeah I know it's not right but it's life in this town,
You either play by the rules or lose your life in this town.
Can you really be harmed here? You certainly will,
Leave now and I'll see you next time you come to Murderville.

“In My Lifetime”(Part 1)

All I ever needed was something I rarely had,
What I rarely had was something hardly shown.
Lies and deception, heartbreak and tears,
I am preparing 2 cry my last river.
If only they could see inside of my fragile heart,
Maybe then my views could be somewhat justified.
I guess the good die young so I wait my turn,
My mind observes a lot so I’ve seen 2 much.
What I think and know could shape this cruel world,
But this crooked society will continue 2 fight me.
Even “crazy” people speak a lot of truth,
But we never see that because all we do is judge.
Maybe I’m a crazy person, who actually knows?
Only God can judge me so I live life content.
Love has come and gone so many times it’s true,
Through the pain my heart felt I still made it through.
You could write a whole book on this life of mine,
Good times, bad times, is what I’ve shared –n- my lifetime.

"If I don't make it 'til morning"

If I should die before the morning appears,
Let my loved ones rejoice but please shed no tears.
My life hasn't been bad but it could've been better,
When it came 2 my father all I had was his letters.
A few pictures, some calls, some visits here and there,
No matter how far away he was, he still showed he cared.
I loved a few and got played by many,
My heart was often broken and I felt so empty.

If I should die before the morning shows it's face,
I pray 2 God that my soul goes 2 a better place.
No more tears, no more hurt, no more fears,
No longer being subjected to racism.
If it's written that I die let me pass when it's right,
Yet I often ask God "Don't let me die 2nite".
I loved all those who loved me and even those who didn't,
If there's any hate-n- my heart I hope that God 4gives it.
Allow my words 2 live on if my time should end,
Please LORD 4give me 4 my sins if I don't make it 'till morning.

“Words From A Revolutionary”

Those who judge me do so 4 many reasons,
Mainly because they don’t understand me.
They hate what they don’t know and fear what is strong,
This is why I fight so hard,
I am more than what they think but nothing less than what I am,
I strive to overthrow what they think is fair,
I fight 4 that one thing we all long 4,
I want freedom, justice and love,
Love 4 myself and love 4 my people,
The mountain top isn’t far to reach,
But every time we get close our own kind pulls down,
Put our minds in place and our money will prosper,
Then take that money and create 4 our seeds,
These are the things we need in life,
I’ve written the worlds, it’s up to y’all to do what’s right.

"In Our Society"

They are the ones that said you have the right,
To say whatever you want to say,
You can do whatever you want to do,
Believe whatever best fits you,
This is what they say!

Once you have violated the standard code of law,
Those rights mentioned before are now new rights,
You then have the right to remain silent,
Anything you say can and will be used against you in a court of law,
If convicted you'll be placed in a facility,
Where you can only do what you are told to do,
Some call it unfair society calls it justice,
Believe what you best fits you,
This is how it is!

The more you make the more they take,
The less you make you're forced to take,
Celebrities can assault, kill their wives and wife's lovers,
Make love to minors on videotapes,
Be charged with molestation; get caught with drugs and weapons,
And see little to no jail time,
What about the celebrities that can't afford a good lawyer,
They go to jail because they defended their CEO,
You helped yourself but let him fry,
Is that fair, some say it is,
What if the average person did these things?
They'd be forced to have a public defender,
The thing is they only defend the poor and middle class public,
But ultimately they don't even work 4 you,
Whether they win, lose or draw,
They get paid and you get injustice,
Is that fair, some say it is,
Believe what best fits you,
This is how it is!

"Who Else But Me?"

Who writes like me and works like me?
Who wakes up everyday prepared to fight like me?
Everyday is something new live your life like me,
Before you sleep take the time to pray at night like me.
Want like me and need like me,
If I cut you don't think you won't bleed like me.
Open your eyes and see like me,
Then tell me how it feels to be like me.
Your mom is strong; your "pops" tries his best,
Your brother idolizes you, is that fair?
Your father cares but he's far away,
Sometimes you want to end it all; that's my life.
Females don't really care 4 you,
But there are a chosen few that's there 4 you,
You're the one everyone calls 4 help,
But no one's there 4 you so you have to save yourself.
You read this and think could this be?
Is this really reality, yeah it is 4 me.

"I Do it 4 You (Why I Cry)"

In my eyes I cry tears,
But the tears I cry aren't normal tears.
I cry 4 all the children who don't have parents,
I cry 4 all the women who are often abused.

In my eyes I cry tears,
But the tears I cry aren't normal tears.
I cry 4 all the men who can't see their kids,
I cry 4 all the innocent people that are in prison.

In my eyes I cry tears,
But the tears I cry aren't normal tears.
I cry 4 many reason but most of all,
I cry 4 all the people who can't cry anymore.

"I Tried"

~And I Try~

To do the very best I can,
But life ain't easy being a young man.
Being black don't change nothin',
Whether you're white or any other color you gotta go through somethin'.
It gets hard I get scarred and the odds,
At times are against me the only one with me,
Is God so with that said I hold my head high,
Even though I fall short it's cool 'cus I tried.

~And I Know~

That everyone won't like me and love me,
Say what you will but only God can judge me.
Push me shove me but nothin' will budge me,
I am what I am and that's all I can be,
Simply a man, a man with dreams,
My words are cinematic it's like I'm writing scenes.
I cry like so many that are ashamed to say it,
My life is quite real and my poetry displays it.
And with all that said I hold my head up high,
Even though I fall short it's cool 'cus I tried.

"Elders Speaking to the Youth"

I've been where you're at,
Seen what you've seen,
Felt what you've touched,
I've dreamed what you've dreamed,
I've laughed like you laugh,
And cried like you cried,
When it's all said and done,
I'll die like you'll die,
Though our lives are at different stages we're playing the same game,
Nothing you feel is new to me 'cus we're one in the same.

"Can't Knock The Hustle"

(Dedicated 2 those who "do what they gotta do")

Catch me if you can but I think you won't,
It's not that I'm too fast you're just too slow.
I do what I do not because I want to,
I do these things because I have to.
Mama's rent is due, I got bills that's past due,
My baby's mother got no job and my baby needs shoes.
I make money the money don't make me,
Gotta find ways to get by but society wants to break me.
Because of my color society hates me,
But I don't trip off them instead it takes me,
To a level much higher than the weed you smoke,
I rarely sleep 'cus dreamin' just leaves you broke.
So until I reach my goal I refuse to stop.
That's why I chill at the spot and that spot is the block.

“All Eyez On Me (Still)”

All eyez are on me so please be advised,
I’ll let you in on secret so don’t be surprised.
This time the revolution will be televised,
On the other hand let’s keep that a surprise.

All eyez are on me so please feel free,
To marvel at the wonderful sight that is me.
Until I die I’ll strive 4 peace,
4 that is the state of mind that is perfect 4 me.

All eyez are on me so it’s cool if you stare,
Go ahead and prejudge me ‘cus of my clothes and hair,
Say what you want and even though it’s not fair,
I know your eyez are on me but guess what I DON”T CARE!

“My Matrix”

I can’t take this,
Why must I face this?
Lord erase this,
It’s like I’m in the matrix.
Why you think is complicated,
In reality is basic,
When it comes to pain,
I often hate to retrace it,
My mind replays it,
I can’t explain it,
My poetry displays it,
In so many ways,
Like a picture that’s painted,
Or a puzzle properly placed,
In a maze type of order,
There’s no way to fake it,
You can’t sketch it or draw it,
You’d simply have to trace it,
Ok, it’s not what you think,
It’s actually worse 4 granted its’ often taken,
Mental images of its end once awakened,
My body’s filled with sweat and I’m alone scared and shaking.
Hold on just wait,
There’s a point to be made,
What we make out to be complicated,
Is so basic,
Until it’s over,
We all must proceed through this matrix.
Whether it’s wrong,
Whether it’s right,
The matrix that I’m in,
Is nothing more than life.

“The Matrix”
(Pt.2 to “My Matrix”)

Trials and tribulations come like bills that are past due,
Stress reflects demonic hands that often grab you.
We seem to pick the wrong people to love and get attached to,
But this is the open scene to a play I call life.
Men loving men or men loving women *and* men,
Women do the same thing, where does the insanity end?
Children grow up without elders to direct them,
Then it’s ironic that elders choose children and molest them.
But those are scenes in the movie we often watch,
A movie that I simply call Life’s Matrix.

"Don't Hate Me"

I can't help that what I do you can't do,
It's not that you can't you just choose not to.
All that hatin' is time and energy wasted,
If you took the energy used 4 hatin' and simply placed it,
Into something positive you'd be surprised,
That right b4 your eyes you could finally make it.
But no you choose to use disrespectful views,
You'll never win that way but it's cool go on and do,
Exactly what you do don't take this as rude,
But with that attitude you're simply bound to lose.
And if that's fine with you, ok, but I refuse,
To run the race of life in a pair of losin' shoes,
That's why I chose to do what I need to do,
In order 4 me to do the things needed to,
Put myself in a position where the time I spent dreamin',
Along with all the schemes will pay off 4 me.
But no matter what I achieve I truly believe,
Haters will do their job and won't lay off of me.
So to them I say with a great delight,
Continue to do your job but you won't block my light.

"Images Of Me"

Every now and again I find myself watching,
Observing as well as becoming strangely connected,
Connected to the sights that my eyes are being focused on,
Those sights are the visions that others created.
With money and a dream those visions are being seen,
4 the world to embrace upon the television and movie screens.
Certain characters touch a certain spot in my heart,
Because I was just like them in a way,
Be it Forrest Gump or the handicapped boy named Radio,
Either scenario I can relate to,
The way they were treated I was treated the same way,
I felt what they felt each and every day.
Even though I'm older nothing has really changed,
I'm still being looked at as if I'm strange.
My eyes often tear because it hurts so bad,
To become so directly connected to images of myself,
How could movie producers recreate my pain,
So vividly 4 the entire world to see?
From being told there were no seats left on the bus 4 me,
To walking around town with my beloved radio,
I am those individuals but I await to see,
If the happy endings they received will take place 4 me.

"Still the Same"

Have you ever wanted to cry but the tears wouldn't fall?
You ever wanted to speak to someone but had no one to call?
You ever prayed to God but didn't think that he hears you?
You ever felt the cold hands of death creeping up near you?
You ever dance with the devil in the pale moonlight?
I have, I do it every day and night of my life.
Have you ever cared 4 someone who didn't care?
When the odds weren't right you tried to make them fair.
Have you ever had someone touch your heart,
Just to hear some bad things that ripped it apart?
You ever dance with the devil in the pale moonlight?
I have, I do it every day and night of my life.

"Memory Lane"

Not only do I walk down this lane everyday,
I live here as well and the pain that I faced,
Made me a stronger person and everyday it rained,
I didn't stay in the house I stayed out and played.
The water set me free so I continued to stay,
In the rain simply playing until my mother would say,
It was time to come in but I really hated to leave,
'cus being out in the rain was like freedom to me.
It gave me the freedom to be as free as I could be,
With the ability to see so clearly I could see,
Any and everything and the air that I would breathe,
Felt so wonderful that it felt just like a dream.
But it was no dream what I was feeling was nice,
I wouldn't trade that feeling or sell it 4 any price.
And I sit on my porch I often smile when it rains,
Until I die I'm staying right here on Memory Lane.

"When A Clown Cries"

It's always sad to see a clown without his smile,
All the joy that he had has been gone 4 a while.
You can find only a small trace of it in his eyes,
In a locked dressing room he often sits and cries.
Who on earth would upset a clown?
Why would someone or something turn his smile to a frown?
He doesn't dance around he just sits and weeps,
He often does that until he's fast asleep.
Traces of make-up are on his pillow and sheets,
He walks with his head down as he walks down the street.
He went from being a clown to becoming a mute,
That's the only things to assume 'cus he no longer speaks.
You can clearly see his pain when you look into his eyes,
I hope you never have to see a clown when he cries.

“Similar Tears”

You ever cried to the point that your eyes felt dry?
I’ve done it many times and they often ask me why?
I’ve cried when I was happy, I’ve cried because of pain,
There was no umbrella large enough to shield me from the rain.
My heart has been broken; my feelings were often hurt,
In the mist of feeling that I wondered what was it worth?
I felt lower than dirt; I was beyond the edge,
I was ready to leap all I needed was a ledge.
I’ve cried 4 all the kids who deal with broken homes,
No one is there to help them so they often feel alone.
I was the same child and at times I still am,
The struggle is never easy being a black man.
Being young and talented doesn’t help matters at all,
There are so many people against me just hoping that I will fall.
You ever cried so much that your eyes felt dry?
I’ve done it many times and those were some of the reasons why.

"Man Of Mystery"

He sits isolated with his face looking so down,
He stays away from crowds and rarely makes a sound.
He is so shy but has a big heart,
The only thing he has in this world is his art.
Art being his poetry; his one true love,
The only thing in this world that makes him happy,
He dreams of being in love; reality shows him his past,
When his heart was often broken he often wears a mask,
His eyes tell a story that's deep indeed,
But he keeps his head down so his eyes can't be seen,
He dresses in dark clothes or jerseys with his hat low,
Some memories are now 4gotten from past years when he once smoked.
Who is this mystery man of whom I speak?
Look no further than who you see 'cus that mystery man is me!

"The Art Of Working"

I work hard all the time,
But *they* don't see,
Work, work, work,
That's all *they* see!
Faster, faster!
That's what *they* yell,
Going home is like heaven,
'cus working is like hell.
If I take a break,
They look funny and mad,
But *they* break all the time,
And that is so sad.
It's cool I'll keep working,
But it's not 4 my health,
I'll have to deal with this drama,
Until I work 4 myself.

"Can't Knock the Hustle (Pt.2)"

In the mist of sorrow and constant pain,
There's little hope 4 2morrow and the constant strain,
That's placed on my brain could drive a man insane,
There's little hope 4 the sun 'cus I constantly see rain,
I try my best to proceed and play the game,
The best way possible spent plenty of time in hospitals,
Looked at by physicians they say my screws are missin',
My heart skips a beat but I won't leave my mission,
I must find a way to receive a gain in pay,
They want me to make less so 4 now I have to play,
Every single day outside on the block,
Constantly movin' stock and watchin' out 4 the cops,
Use tools to build then proceed to run blocks,
Quarterback the work my passes never stops,
If so I'll cut my hand off before they stop a handoff,
Pitch it to my running backs then they do a flee flicker,
Me I'm quicker a small man with dreams,
My aim is to get cream- Can't Knock the Hustle.

“I Do It 4 You (Pt.2)”

Take a nice look into these blood shot eyes,
Everyday is a struggle but yet I still survive.
Organized chaos describes my life,
What they view as wrong I think is right,
4 those without a voice,
those who have nothing,
those that need a change,
those who struggle daily,
4 the kids who feel lost,
without a soul to turn to,
who come from a broken home,
4 THEM I WRITE!
And 4 those who feel trapped,
Beat down and depressed,
I’ll gladly go to war 4 them,
And 4 THEM I WRITE!

"Judge Not"

(Dedicated 2 the spirit of racism)

I cry like the rest of y'all
I feel pain like the rest of y'all
But why is it that you judge me,
When I don't judge none of y'all
You show me no love because I'm different,
You say that you're better than me,
How is it I can't judge you,
But you constantly judge me?

I dream like you dream,
I wish like you wish,
I hope 4 some of the same things you hope 4,
Yet 4 some reason you don't accept me.
You think I'm a menace 2 everything you hold sacred,
Why is it that you are afraid of me?
I don't fear you because I love you,
And somewhere inside of you, you admire me.

I was created by the same power that created you,
There is no way that you can deny me of who I am.
Say what you want and do what you want 2 me,
But my spirit shall never be broken or altered.
What you feel is something that was taught 2 you,
And I pray that you see the light one-day
When you finally realize that how you feel is wrong,
I'll be here 2 greet you with open arms.

I'm not a menace and I have the same rights as you,
When times are hard I will fight just like you.
I cry like you cry, love you like you love,
In the end will my life ends I'll die like you'll die.
B4 you judge me look inside of yourself,
Take a close look and then fix what's broken.
These words were spoken because you feel the need 2 judge me,
You judge me because you're afraid, afraid that you might respect me and love me.

Chapter III: Love (The Good, Bad and In-between)

"How Do I (Say Goodbye?)"

(Dedicated 2 those that can relate)

How do I say goodbye?
At times I don't know
The tears in my eyes
Can surely show
What I feel inside
But it's all because of u
Nites I sit crying
All because of u
Where do I start with this?
Allow me 2 see
Where things went wrong
With u and me
U said u cared but in the end u lied
Hurt me and hurt me
And apart of me died
How do I say goodbye?
Should I just pack up and leave?
Kiss u once more then step out with my heart in my sleeve
Do u really give a damn?
No, wait b4 u speak
I'm not through yet
And b4 I hit the streets
Let me tell u something
That u may not be aware of
I may not know everything about everything
But I do know about love
It shouldn't hurt while you're in it
But with u it did
It's like a war that couldn't be won
So many ways it slid
Further and further down till it couldn't go anymore
Just walk away from me now
I don't want 2 see u no more
NO, Please wait
I love u so much
I miss your smile
And the warmth of your touch
But u lied 2 me!
Over and over again
U asked me is it ok if we remain friends?
ARE U CRAZY IN YOUR SCALP?
Did u bump your head?
Have u paid attention 2 anything that I've said?

What we had was good at first but u made it bad
Trust became broken and fragile
And now I feel so sad
I can't believe it
U played me as if I was a kid
How do I say goodbye?
I think I just did.

"Can I?"

(After the Break-Up)

Hold up Ms. Lady,
I couldn't help but notice,
Out the corner of my eye,
The most beautiful sight,
So if it's alright can I talk with u?
We can make this a convo 2 go so can I walk with u?
What u smiling 4?
Do u think I'm funny?
U got some pretty eyes lady,
I'm wondering if maybe,
I can ask u something,
Would I be 2 forward,
If I said that I need u,
No, not in that way,
But we can take it there,
Sike, I'm just jokin',
But really I was just hopin',
2 engage in a convo without saying, "Aye can I holla at u?"
Baby I ain't no playa so I ain't gotta pop my collar at u,
I got madd money but I ain't throwin' no dollars at u,
Cuz any woman with a brain can get things herself,
I can see the look in ur eyes hold up, don't speak,
Somebody did u wrong,
And left u weak,
Said he was working late but he was out on the creep,
Spending time on the grind messing with madd dimes,
Grabbin' at ur friend's behinds,
Time after time,
So u spent hours upon hours with ur pillow just crying,
Yea I know the feeling lady,
I just got out of some stuff,
I had 2 find a way 2 say goodbye,
Cuz enough was enough,
Oh, what did I say?
Well something like this,
"How do I say goodbye?
I think I just did"
No it didn't hurt at all,
Cuz it had 2 be done,
She wasn't right 4 me anyways,
But that's all alone,
Back 2 u Ms. Lady love,
With that smile so bright,

If you're not busy lata on,
Can we chill 4 the nite,
Watch a lil movie,
Cuddle on the couch,
If u give me a chance,
I can show u what love is all about,
I ain't a doctor but I do have madd patience,
U only live once,
So what's the use in waiting?
Toss that number at me lady,
I can't deny,
I was attracted when I saw u,
But not cuz of ur hips and thighs,
It was ur scent and ur eyes that had me lost like whoa,
I looked at u and I knew that I had 2 know,
What kinda person u are,
And what u like 2 do,
Time ain't 4ever baby so it's all on u,
What u wanna do,
U wanna ride with me,
It's whatever baby girl I can ride with u,
Let's exchange numbers,
Things will happen if u try,
I can be what u want me 2,
I'm just askin' can I?

"Cry With Me"

When the pain is 2 much,
Will you cry with me?
Will you lie in the bed,
Side by side with me?
Hold me in your arms,
Keep me safe from harm.
When no one else is there,
Let me know you're there.
Is that 2 much 2 ask?
If so, you can leave.
If your love 4 me is true,
I hope you can see,
I'm not saying appear –n- court,
And lie 4 me,
Jump in the way of a bullet,
Or even die 4 me,
Simply stay with me,
Watch time fly with me.
And when the pain becomes 2 much,
Simply cry with me.

“Deep”

If I were unable to produce tears,
Would you cry 4 me?
IF death came my way,
Would you die 4 me?
Be it a cop or the judge.
Would you lie 4 me?
When we’re having problems,
Could you try 4 me?
My love is your love,
My pain is your pain,
No matter how much we lose,
In time we’ll soon gain.
Everyday can’t be sunny,
So we have 2 see rain,
Stress comes with the package,
But we have 2 maintain.
Hold me like I hold you,
Never 4get the things I’ve told you.
Love me like I miss you,
Miss me like I dream of you,
Cry 4 me like I try 4 you,
In a sense die 4 me like I’d die 4 u.

"Love Don't Love Me"

(A Song 4 my heart)

I trusted in you but you never cared,
I always thought that you would be there.
All you ever did was halfway love me,
I'm lost because love don't love me anymore.

As the days fade away so does my hopes,
You just keep playing with my heart and mind.
I'm hurt because you're never there for me,
I'm lost because love don't love me anymore.

Sometimes I wonder if I'm the one to blame,
Could it be that we were never meant to be?
I thought I would be fine but I'm dying inside,
I'm lost because love don't love me anymore.

"Another Chance 2 Love"

If only it were possible to love again,
I'd surely do it in a heartbeat,
So much pain hit my heart and now it's hard,
At this point I'm not sure I could open up.
I know I want love but does love want me?
And if so, then why does it seem to taunt me?
Why do certain memories seem to haunt me?
Questions are often asked but where are the answers?
I'll continue to rebuild and I know one day,
This thing called love will come my way.
If only it were possible to love again,
I'd surely jump at the chance and do it in a heartbeat.

"Because Of U"

(Written 4 my cousin "Sleepy")

If only I had one more chance,
Just another opportunity 2 hold your hand.
You and only you could ignite my flame,
The sound of your name could erase my pain.
But those days are done because you left one day,
Once you walked out of my life you took my breath away.
Just when I thought I was over you,
Our paths crossed again right out of the blue.
At first I didn't realize it was you,
But when I looked again I clearly noticed you.
As you spoke I didn't know what 2 say 2 you,
My mind replayed all of the good days with you.
Damn I wish I could've stayed with you,
The person I am now was made by you.
Without a doubt my heart was slain by you,
Why oh why must I feel so sad?
The rock on your finger made me feel so bad,
So many things I wanted 2 say but I couldn't speak.
There's no reason 2 lay down, I know I wouldn't sleep,
I cant lie about my feelings 'ma that's not me.
But the person you're in love with is not me,
I cant say I'm over you 'cus that's not me.
But holdin' on 2 lost love I can not do,
I must pick up my heart and then carry on,
'cus there's no use in loving when you're loving alone

“What Love Can Do”

Damn I feel so crazy right now,
Your hugs got me feeling so crazy right now.
Your lips got me wishing you’ll stay with me now,
Your eyes got me hoping you’ll lay with me now.
It’s not hard to tell from reading this,
That this is what love can do 2 a person.

“When N Love”

The sun shines bright and the stars are beautiful,
Even a stormy day seems quite enjoyable.
Everything is everything and the world is great,
Those things take place when you’re in love.

Phone calls last 4ever and the talks are wonderful,
Love letters are often written for no reason at all.
Flowers and poetry express what you feel,
All these things happen when you’re in love.

"You Bitch!"

(Dedicated 2 Love)

Damn I really hate you!
Don't talk to me anymore I said I hate you!
I swear to God I really love you,
Bitch, bitch, you're such a bitch!

Your definition of truth ain't the same as mine,
We both have watches but we're on different times.
I could call you many things but I'll call you this,
Bitch, bitch, you're such a bitch!

You've cared before but not now it seems,
All you do is now is destroy my dreams.
You are what you are so u can't deny it,
Bitch, bitch, you're such a bitch!

"Run Away"

If its not 2 much trouble
Will u do me a favor?
Just give me your hand
Don't worry I will explain later
Just please give me your hand
And let us travel 2 a place
Where smiles will be the only things
Placed upon your face
If u trust me then give me your hand
And run away with me
I'll pick you up in the evening
So later u can lay with me
U can spend the whole day with me
If all goes well
I hope that u will stay with me
We can go 2 church 2gether
And then u can pray with me
Hook up a game or something
Maybe u will play with me
All I ask is that u love me
Even though I'm not perfect
I promise if u hang in there
It will all be worth it
If we play our cards right
We might just find
Happiness and love
At times in my mind
All I see is u
Well really I see us
Building on love and trust
And commitment is a must
What we have won't die
As long as we both try
And keep it real with each other
And the man up high
Must receive all the glory
4 placing us here
As long we trust in him
There's no need 2 fear
Let me rid u of your pain
By merely speaking
Let my words become the shelter
Your heart has been seeking
During the coldest nights

Allow my love 2 warm u
Like bees, at any given time
My love could swarm u
But let me warn u
If I should change at times
Its only because true love
Is hard 2 find
And I have played the love game
And paid the cost
But its better 2 have loved and lost
Then 2 have never loved at all
And what we have feels good don't it?
Lovin u a lil bit more wouldn't hurt would it?
I think not and if so
If u want me gone
I'll get ghost
With my heart in my sleeve
I hope 2 achieve
Nothing more that the honor
Of having you with me
Before I let u leave me
I'd 1st let bullets fly and hit me
Square in the heart
Cuz without u I'd have nothing
Bring your body over here
And let me grab something
I don't carry knives
But I'm sure 2 stab something
In the heat of passion
I'm bound 2 squeeze and touch something
Make the feeling long lasting
Guaranteed 2 lust nothing
Take it slow
Make it go
Do u like?
Tell me so
If u don't
Let me know
But I can tell
Your body shows
All of the evidence
Of no foul play
When I entered your residence
And I could tell by your hesitance
U felt a lil pain
But then I surely cured you

Had u twisted
The things we inflicted
Felt good, aren't u glad u insisted
We go further
Ease up I won't hurt ya
Take a deep breath, relax we had fun and
I'm glad u ran away with me
But it was jus our minds that did the running

"My Wish"

There are so many words I want 2 speak
But I'm afraid you won't listen
When the sun rises and sets
It is you that I'm missing
A lonely reality often gives me vivid visions
All I see is mental pictures
Of warm hugs and kisses
In just a short time
This heart of mine
Has finally begun 2 mend
All traces of sadness
Has been brought 2 an end
Where do I begin?
I know it starts from within
My thoughts drift n the wind
And when it's done
I start again
Is it me?
Is it you?
Could there possibly be "us"?
Who can I trust?
When pain has turned my heart 2 rust
But because of you it shines again
Love is a door
That we are scared 2 open
But if we don't try
We'll end up not knowin'
And not showin'
Anyone any type of affection
It's our hearts we're neglectin'
All I need are the proper directions
N2 your heart
N2 your world then manifestin'
A cold heart
N2 warm love, I'm electin'
2 give you all the love
That I've collected
What was once dead
Has now resurrected
Will u be mine?
N my mind
You already are
As bright as the stars
I wish I may

I wish I might
If it's possible
Be granted the wish
That I wish 2nite
Despite the outcome
I will take what's due
A wise man once said
"To thyne own-self be true"
True words from William Shakespeare
Let's take minutes and hours
Days and months
And commence 2 make years
If you're scared
We can take fears
And be rid of that
Later on we can smile about what we did n fact
I know you're special
Let's go, take it slow
Water the seed of love
And then let it grow
If you cry, then I'll cry
Your tears are my tears
Your pain is my pain
We lose and then gain
Whenever my heart speaks
I write what's true
Anytime I make wishes
I wish on you

"The Ones 2 Blame"

I know I said I would speak of her,
I try my hardest to keep from speaking to her.
Most folks that know her don't see me,
Just so I wont be reminded of her.
Why fight the fact that I still love her?
But it's obvious she has outgrown me.
What I did 4 her can't be replaced,
But I think she found a way 2 do that.
She, at one point was someone I loved,
But maturity is something that split us apart.
Was it really my fault or was it simply her?
Maybe, just maybe, it was both of us!

"A Cry From My Heart"

I'm not sure how 2 explain what I feel
but I guess I have 2
When it comes 2 u
I cant rest till I have u
It seems I have so many questions 2 ask u
4 every one that comes 2 mind
it seems like I have 2 ask 2
Mysterious love of my life
may I please unmask u?
So I can see the real u
then proceed 2-grab u
Love is surrounded by fiction
but has some facts 2
What is it about me
that seems 2 attract u?
I want 2 feel what u feel
and be one with you
I want 2 smile when u cant
and cry the tears u cant shed
Its like I dream of u
cause I cant see u
All I want is u
and 2 be with u
With a heart full of love
I sat here and wrote this
U mean alot 2 me
and u can quote this
Through my words and actions
I hope 2 show this
How I feel isn't new
so u should already know this
I'm giving u a piece of my heart
and I want u 2 hold it
If I didn't mean these words
this poem would be hopeless...
2 be continued...

"Full Yet Still Hungry"

2 truly express my most intimate emotions,
I'd have to climb the Grand Canyon without breaking a sweat.
Which means it's impossible to tell you,
May I can, I can, I can show you,
How you make me feel 4ever blessed and completed,
Totally satisfied yet I yearn 4 more.
Let me stuff myself until my belly is full,
Belly meaning my heart and I'm full from you.

~Yes I'm full, but may I have some more? ~

Take me 2 the place where you discovered the art,
The art of operating on wounded hearts.
How did you manage to perfectly manifest,
Into every single piece of the perfect fantasy I've wanted?
Each cookie b4 dinner I consumed,
Had my appetite spoiled but I continued to eat.
I ate until I felt like passing out,
Passing out from overdosing,
Taking too much too soon, I could get sick,
Well let me become ill, I must take this chance,
To consume your food until my belly is full,
Belly meaning my heart and it's safe to say,
I've done it; my fantasy is now a reality,
I've engulfed too much, I'm full but please,
Give me more!
I'm full but may I have some more?

Some more of you, some more of your love,
But yet I must I reach out 4 another plate.

~Yes I'm full, but may I have some more? ~

"The Art Of Giving Someone A Chance"

As my mind wonders into a miraculous environment,
I become more and more involved,
Involved and completely at ease with knowing,
Knowing that you somehow, someway,
Captured my emotions and every in depth thought,
You, you, you are those thoughts.
The one image that sooths and quenches my emotional thirst,
The ultimate high, my outstanding motivation,
The person who gives me strength,
But one look into those eyes easily cripples me.
How do I find the way?
To somehow, someway,
Tell you that I adore you so much,
I want to somehow, somehow,
Show you that I'm amazed by you,
I find my spirit at peace when you're with me.
As I wish upon the brightest star,
Hoping that someway, somewhere, and somehow,
I could construct a scheme to make you,
Not make in the sense of using forceful actions,
Or make in the sense of creating,
But make in the innocent and most magical way of realizing,
That our meeting was not a coincidence,
But an inevitable encounter perfectly constructed,
To teach, grow, embrace and learn from.
With open minds and lonely hearts involved,
It becomes evident that we might be,
That one thing that is known throughout the universe,
That, of which a genie can't create,
That, of which our grandparents posses,
That, of which we all love 2 see,
That, of which we all love 2 read about,
That thing that begins a poet's quest,
That thing that poets write about,
That thing that we can't live life without,
That thing that makes r & b music make complete sense,
We could be each other's love.

We could complete our long and painful quest,
A quest to have the *one*,
The one you think of when you're alone,
The one that you talk to for hours on the phone,
The one who gives slight butterflies in your tummy,
That one that you watch TV with,

The one that you cuddle with,
The one that you love to love,
And at times even love to hate,
The one that you can't live life without,
The one you believe has helped you find your meaning,
Your meaning and purpose in loving,
The first face you see in the morning,
And the last face you see at night,
The crème in my coffee,
The stars in my sky,
The love in my heart,
And the spark in my eyes,
How can I simply find the way?
To open up and just somehow,
Somehow say, say that,
I honestly believe with all of me,
And all that was used to make me,
That you might be, you could easily be,
Nothing more than my perfect match,
What we don't try,
We may never experience,
What we don't leave,
Will always remain,
What we don't explore,
We may never know,
If we don't trust ourselves,
We may never grow,
A closed mouth never gets fed,
And a full stomach puts us to sleep,
Blind eyes rarely hear a trusting heart,
Past situations replay in our present,
Which can ultimately shape our future.

The guilty ones are memories but we often commit the mistake,
Of unintentionally convicting the next one we feel 4.
Convicting them of things we think they did,
Or convicting them before they do anything,
All because the apple fell from the tree,
We can't open up and trust another.
I've been there so I can relate 2 it,
But the next person could help you find you're way through it.
I just somehow, somewhere, and someway,
Wish that I could get you 2 see,
That I believe in my heart and all that makes me,
And all that was used in the creating of me,
That if you open up and proceed to trust,

Trust those butterflies and that one thing,
That thing that lightens up your voice a little bit,
That thing that triggers your mind 2 think,
2 think of that one person that makes you,
realize that somewhere, someway and somehow,
deep, deep, deep inside of you,
you actually managed to do this thing,
this thing called missing that person.

That thing that makes you find a way,
Find a way or find some ways,
To do nothing less but maybe more,
But all in all, simply see that person.
Convict me now because I must turn myself in,
Because I am without further deliberation found guilty.
Guilty of feeling all of these things,
I feel these things because I care about you.
And if you can say that you can't relate,
To not one of these things as they pertain to me,
I'll die more than a thousand deaths,
Only to resurrect and die again,
But if you feel at least one of these things I've said,
It's obvious that you should slowly drop the wall,
The wall that keeps you safe from harm,
Safe from harm and safe from love,
4 I have dropped mine and looked over it,
and what I saw was simply you.
If only you could do the same thing too,
I could be standing on the other side.
Ready to help with paying the bills,
Ready to help cook and clean the dishes,
Ready to not leave the toilet seat up,
Ready to explain the ins and outs of sports,
Ready to listen and turn away from the game,
Ready to make you breakfast in bed,
Ready to help during the pregnancy,
Ready to hold your hand during labor,
Ready to help raise the baby or babies we may have,
Ready to be more than your "baby's daddy",
Ready to make you more than my "baby's mama",
But instead making you my life long partner.
Hold me, mold me, and make of me what you want,
Because right now you are already everything I've ever wanted.
Before we get here we need one simple tool,
Once that tool is found we may then build,
Build towards a relationship founded and run off,

Love, trust, and communication,
I'm not asking 4 the world,
All I want,
Is 4 you 2 do something 4 me,
Just give me your hand.

Give me your hand once the trust is there,
Trust in me like I believe in you,
Believe in me like you believe in love,
I want to take you to the mountaintop,
So we could leave the world behind,
I plan to do this as soon as possible,
Just as soon as you give me your hand,
So as I reach out to receive your hand,
I need to know something,
I need to know if somewhere, someway and somehow,
You can simply find it in your heart,
To do one thing and one thing first,
And that is nothing more,
Than give me your hand.

“If I”

~If I~

Could magically reverse the universe,
And create a time frame that connected you and I,
Any and everything would be yours to name,
Time would stop completely when I look into your eyes.

~If I~

Had it my way I’d have it all,
Which simply means all I would have is you,
Nothing more, nothing less, just simply you,
The greatest treasures of the world would be a minimal gain.

~If I~

Could only open my mouth and say,
That I think of you every night and day,
If only you knew that my feelings run deep,
Just knowing that you know would make my circle complete.

“Paradise”

Why do I feel the way that I feel?
Is it my imagination or could it be real?
What you have now you say you don’t want,
So why do you still hold on to it?
You see what makes you happy but I don’t know why,
You rather keep what makes you cry,
I want to give you something you don’t have,
And that’s the gift of being happy.
Don’t convict me of what your past love did,
Me and him are two different guys,
Just open up and give me your hand,
And together we’ll find paradise.

“Any Other Way”

Tell me love do you trust me and if you do,
Will you give me a chance to prove to you?
That you are the only thought that crosses my mind,
And I wouldn’t have it any other way.

Tell me love do you think of me?
And if you do tell me what do you think?
4 some reason I find myself amazed by you,
and I wouldn’t have it any other way.

Tell me love why do you hesitate,
When you know we can be together?
If you want to take your time that’s fine with me,
And I wouldn’t have it any other way.

"Lovers Lane"

Take my hand and together we'll journey to a place,
Where teardrops won't be allowed upon your face.
Let's go 2 a place where you'll find pure bliss,
The excitement of ecstasy can be found with one kiss.
What do you say love, can you hang 4 a few?
I'm tryin' 2 step with you I ain't thinking about my crew.
The way I c it there's a fork in the road,
What lies on either side only the Lord knows.
And don't view this as rude but I think you're fine,
Every part of you is perfect you're one of a kind.
I'd trade any and everything 2 make you mine,
I can c it in your eyes you've been hurt many times.
You're not alone I 2 have felt some pain,
I keep telling myself I'll never love again.
That's a lie 'cus all hearts need a match,
But at times we lose track because our feelings get too attached.
Enough about me let's get back 2 you,
And if you give me a try we might create something called us.
This is your chance so love hop on the bus,
Love can't occur without communication and trust.
I understand that you don't know me,
But I can tell there are some things that you want 2 show me.
There's no need 2 worry but we all get scared,
Love often creeps on us when we're rarely prepared.
With all that being said let's proceed 2 exchange,
Names and numbers and journey on,
Journey on to that wonderful and fun filled place,
With your hand in mine we'll journey down lovers lane.

“Infatuated”

(Dedicated 2 Love)

The 1st time I took a look at you,
I can c why so many folks are hooked on you.
At times people mess up when they look 4 you,
They rarely find what they thought they wanted.
Even I made mistakes being around you,
I was so shy and nervous when I found you.
Then you left and returned at a different time,
You always put a twist on my mind.
At times you’re often hard to find,
But I won’t stop lookin’ until you’re mine.
Why is it that I yearn 4 you?
When mistakes are made it’s true I often learn from you.
I c your face when I’m sleeping,
You dry my eyes when I’m weeping.
At times I look 4 you in all the wrong faces,
Waste precious time in all the wrong places.
Because of you I do some crazy things,
And if believing in you is wrong I don’t want 2 be right.
You are the ultimate high that keeps me captivated,
You have no clue of what you do 2 me.

"Come Back and Stay"
(A Song 4 Love)

Love sweet love, why do u run?
Why do u run from me?
All I want to do is be one with u,
Why won't u come to me?
When it's cold outside or even when it's too hot,
U make everything fine.
I could probably have anything I want,
But all I want is 4 u to be mine.

Love sweet love, why are u gone?
Why aren't u here with me?
All I want to do is be one with u,
But I'm alone feeling misery,
When the world is against me and the chips are down,
U make everything fine.
I could probably have anything I want,
But all I want is 4 u to stay.

"Got-Damn You"

How do I create the right words?
Each statement must perfectly flow together.
To just simply state the undying facts,
That my feelings 4 you are more than unconditional,
On the border of traditional and spiritual,
There's only one way to define my thoughts,
You seem to,
You somehow,
Someway you make me feel,
Like I can fly to the highest mountain,
Achieve the most prominent award,
When I look at you as you walk by,
Your beauty brings tears to my eyes.
As your enchanting aroma proceeds passed me,
All I can say is simply this,
GOT-DAMN YOU!

"Bye-Bye Love"

What was once reality must become the past,
I honestly was convinced that what we had would last.
Images replay of what could have possibly been,
But those images float away like a kite in the wind.
In life we find people then lose them in the end,
Maybe what we're losing is simply ourselves.
I wanted to love you but you chose to run,
You broke my heart and must've thought it was fun.
Heartache and pain, heartbreak and tears,
They've been in my life throughout my short years.
You seemed so right, you seemed so sweet,
Why did *my* feelings have to be so deep?
I hate you but only because I love,
Even though it hurts to do so I still continue to love you.
I must be a fool 4 trying to care,
Loving a person who was hardly there.
You were around when it benefited you,
But if I needed you, you had things to do.
I was treated like some type of toy,
You only played with me whenever you were bored.
I opened my heart but I must now shut the door,
In order 4 me to grow I can't love you anymore.

“Can We Talk?

U ever felt like during the mist of,
So much pain like your heart’s being ripped up?
All the things that you think of,
Which further makes you realize what you’re sick of,
So many times u said it wont be me again but then you…. slipped up,
Situations were often flipped up,
At times it feels hard 2 go on,
I feel weak but I have 2 be strong,
(Don’t stop homie keep on)
I thought it was love,
We fit like a fresh pair of gloves,
I was caught up in love’s web but I felt smaller than Spud,
She did me dirtier than mud,
This is way beyond crud,
She grabbed my heart, held it, then preceded to pull the plug,
And just when I thought I had enough,
She looked at me and smiled then gave me a hug,
Once again I fell deep into the matrix,
This is far from being basic,
She always found a way 2 keep my heart racin’
If love was a car I had 2 race it,
(Homie just face it),
Yeah I know but from the very first glance,
All I wanted was half of a chance,
We tried 2 fight it but our eyes danced,
Didn’t take much b4 we both dropped our pants,
Love making like a merry go round,
Goin’ in circles oops did I do that like Urkel,
She often said its cool baby there will be times like this,
Mama warned me and said there would be times like this,
BBD said it best when I was a child,
“Don’t fall 4 a big butt and a smile”,
That girl was, and still is 2 this very day…Poison,
And I got infected with it,
I was the best one she could’ve had,
No one was better than,
The one who could ease her pain I was her medicine,
But nothing can cure what u cant diagnose,
She said no 2 me but let other cats go buy her clothes,
I loved her seed like he was my seed,
I was happy when I heard she was havin’ my seed,
But was it really, nah it couldn’t possibly be true,
That she would do what I heard she did,
Having second thoughts about who fathered the kid,

I let it run off my head, I ain't bout 2 be bothered,
Won't catch me on Maury talking bout "you're not the father",
That's 4 suckas, I was trained 2 be tougher,
Didn't have no bigger brother, I learned that from my mother,
But the more I started hearin' things,
It hit me hard like this motherfucker!
No she didn't, yeah she did, but what if they lyin'?
Roll up and let my thoughts start flyin',
Shed tears 2 the point where I was tired of cryin',
No denyin' my heart was slowly dyin',
And I wanted 2 go wit it,
She said things that normally I would've caught but I chose 2 go wit it,
This thing was far from a tight beat but I chose 2 flow wit it,
Our relationship was like a game of hide and go get it,
She would let a cat smash, hop in the shower fast,
Hide the evidence then I would go hit it,
The time came when it all hit me and I felt like Popeye,
I just couldn't stands no more,
This wasn't small like Pluto but not as big as Bluto,
Either which way the spinach helped me finish,
I'm over it as best as I can be,
But I'm human so I can be,
In some ways tempted 2 miss,
The warm hug and kiss,
That phat ass I gripped,
The way it felt so good whenever I dipped and slipped,
Never mind b4 my mind slips,
Into another heartbreaking heart racing episode,
Thanks 4 listenin' I know y'all had enough,
I better let u go.

"A Love (To Call My Own)"

All I see everyday is the same ol' thing,
Everyone's all happy with someone to hold.
Everybody has someone to kiss and hug,
But as 4 me I don't have a single person to love.
How come I have to be the one that's all alone?
Is there a reason why love won't love me back?
I can't stand the fact that I'm always hurtin',
I'm tired of listening to love songs at night.
The only things I can love are the words you read,
These words honestly speak the truth of me.
I wouldn't mind if someone could find the time,
To pick up the phone and call me 'cus I'm on their mind.
Or how about if someone took the time to say,
That I was the one they missed 2day.
I would love a hug or a kiss sometimes,
I would to hold hands from time to time.
Maybe I did something way back in the day,
Which has caused the universe to turn this way.
So many nights spent just looking at the phone,
Waiting 4 it to ring, I'm so alone.
Where is the love that I write about?
Does it only exist in the lines I write?
Why me is the question that I often ask,
I guess in time I'll find my love.

"What a Wonderful Place"

Let us go 2 a place where love dwells,
N a tyme that never stops and the sky is always blue,
The birds always sing and the air is always clean,
Let us go 2 a place like that.

Let us go 2 a place where hearts match,
N a tyme that never stops and the stars shine bright,
Not a cloud in the sky and the weather is right,
Let us go 2 a place like that.

"N Response"

You tell me you love me,
You love me and you love me some more,
I can recall telling myself i wouldn't do this no more,
But once again here i am walking back thru the door,
Hoping i won't have 2 go thru all the heartbreak no more,
With love comes happiness and then the pain comes of course,
The day you walked away from me it's like my heart hit the floor,
I told myself this can't be and 2 the heavens i swore,
I would find a way 2 make it work lettin' it be torn,
Wasn't part of my equation it's you I adore,
On late nights I miss you sittin' behind closed doors,
It's you that excite me I can never be bored,
Loving you is easy it doesn't feel like a chore,
When it comes 2 why I love you 2 be honest it's more,
Than your physical appearance or the great intercourse,
It's like my heart sings 4 u 2 the point where it's hoarse,
Mama can finally be easy and just give you the torch,
What we have came fast some might say it was forced,
If it ain't broke don't fix it just let it take it's course,
I love you more with each second, each minute and every hour,
When it comes 2 keeping you happy all of my power,
Will be used 2 do that let my love just shower,
Over you until the day that I die just know that I,
Need nothing else 'cus everything I want is in u,
And everything means nothing if I don't have you,
I know its crazy baby,
But you're my baby maybe,
I can show you how I feel inside I often try,
And maybe it's not good enough its get rough,
When my mind don't work quick enough,
Like when you say u want 2 see me but ain't got a way,
My mind didn't think quick enough 4 me 2 say,
Don't sweat it mama let me drive 2 you and spend the day,
I'll make it up 2 u I promise till my dying day,
If I can be with anyone boo I hope it's you,
In response 2 your phone call baby I love u 2.

"My Question 2 U"

I'm losing my way,
I'm losing my edge,
I'm falling deeper,
Deeper,
Deeper in2 this thing,
This thing is love,
And I'm falling deeper in it with you.

I'm losing my focus,
I'm losing my sense,
I'm falling deeper,
Deeper in2 this thing,
This thing is love,
And I'm falling deeper in it with you.

But are you feeling the same way?
Or is it something you think is the right thing 2 say?
Are you falling deeper,
Deeper,
Deeper in2 this thing?
This thing is love,
Are you in it with me?
That is the question.

"All N My Head"

U r 2 me like nothing else on earth,
A treasure 4 the world 2 see,
Your eyez, your size, your lipz, your touch,
I just can't get u out of my mind.

Every second that passes makez me fall deeper,
Deeper n a place called n love with u,
Your warmth, your thoughtz, the way u walk,
I just can't get u out of my mind.

If only u felt just a piece of my feelingz,
Maybe then you'd see what I feel 4 u,
Your hair, your smile, the way u talk,
I just can't get u out of my mind.

“Just-n-Case”

If I could simply tell you that I love you now,
Not then, not later, but right this instant.
You make the sun’s rays look a dull light bulb,
I’m telling you this now just in case later doesn’t come.

If I could simply hold you once more,
Not before, not after, but at this time.
Your touch is as soft as a kiss from an angel,
I’m telling you this now just in case later doesn’t come.

If only I could look right into your eyes,
I’m not lookin’ beyond you, I’m lookin’ right at you.
Your eyes are like the doorway into heaven’s gates,
I’m telling you this now just in case later doesn’t come.

Chapter IV: Give Me Peace

“Give Me Peace”

Give me peace!
Please allow me 2 breathe.
No I don’t wish 2 talk,
I’d rather sit alone in silence.
Don’t view me as rude,
I’m just not in a good mood.
Once this mood passes,
I will joke with everyone,
But 4 now let me be,
And give me peace!

"Cries of a sinner"

Have you ever heard the cries of sinner?
Have you ever walked in the same shoes as a sinner?
With power in my heart I wrote these words,
All in hopes to prove a fact,
We all seem to judge and often throw stones,
But here is a statement that's very true.
He or she, who has never sinned,
My only then throw the first stone.
I've heard the endless cries of a sinner,
It often haunts me because it sounds so familiar.
Then I realized why those cries were familiar,
The cries I heard were coming from my soul!

“Not 2nite”

Before I lay me down to sleep,
I pray the lord my soul to keep.
Tomorrow might not come so I wait my time,
I can truly say I’ve seen it all in my lifetime.
Death comes my way but decides to pass,
It mocks me daily ‘cus I can hear its’ laugh.
Why fear something I cannot see?
But that doesn’t mean that it can’t be.
So I ask God to let me die when it’s right,
But at the same time I ask that its not 2nite.

“Peace and Freedom”

Give me peace or let me die,
I can’t lie continue to live in a world of chaos.
Give me peace right here and right now,
And if you can’t grant me that then let me die.

Give me freedom or let me die,
I can’t continue to live in a world that’s a prison.
Give me freedom right here and right now,
And if you can’t grant me that then let me die.

“Knock, Knock, Knock!”

Knock, knock, knock!
Who goes there?
A voice soon replied,
“It is I.
I have come to help you,
Because it was my name you called,
I have come to pick you up,
Because you’ve seemed to have fallen.”
Knock, knock, knock!
Who goes there?
A voice soon replied,
“It is I again.
I have come to save you,
Because it seems you’re lost”,
Then it hit me,
The voice that I heard was the LORD.

"N The Eyes Of God" (Part 1)

Black man, black man, please don't cry,
White man, white man just open your eyes.
We were all created by a higher power,
Son honestly we have no reason 2 fight.
God created us in his own image,
And we all know that God is perfect.
Though we're not perfect he still loves us,
That can be seen if we look with his eyes.

"The Prayer of a Lost Soul"

LORD please just give me a sign,
Open my eyes to love so I won't be blind.
Release the demons that surround my heart,
I want to get to know you but where do I start?

LORD please just give me your love,
Become one with my life like a hand and glove.
Release the anger that sits in my mind,
I want to talk to you, all I need is your time.

LORD please just give me peace,
Find someway to make my pain decrease.
Release my pride and open your arms,
Embrace me with your love and keep me safe from harm.

AMEN

"My Angel"(Part 1)
(Dedicated to God's Spirit)

It feels like God sent me an angel,
But I was 2 blind 2 see.
Everywhere I decided 2 go,
That angel came with me.

It felt like God sent me an angel,
From the heavens above,
No matter how hurt I felt,
That angel showed me love.

It felt like God sent me an angel,
Who always stayed true,
It took a while 4 me 2 notice,
But that angel was you.

"Speaking to God"

I thank you Lord 4 all you've done,
Without you my life would have no meaning,
You are the one that opens my eyes,
It's you that dries my eyes whenever I cry.
Please 4give me 4 the wrongs that I did in my life,
I want to change; all I need is to c the light,
So with that said as I lay me down to sleep,
I meant every word, now my prayer's complete.

“Another Chance To Dance”

Everyday is the same,
Nothing has changed,
I’m still the same,
Doing the same things,
I still look 4 Christ knowing HE is the light,
Yet I still dance with the devil in the pale moonlight.
That’s what I do every single day,
And when the sun goes down I do it every night.
Whether it’s wrong or right this is what I do,
Is there a method to my madness, at times I have no clue.
Every time my eyes open God gives me another chance,
Yet the devil and me always find a way to dance.

"Peace (The only way 4 me)"

Let me c what I need 2 c,
Let me be where I need 2 be,
My attitude doesn't reflect my gratitude,
I know I have a lot 2 be grateful 4,
Teardrops fall like raindrops until puddles are formed,
To some it seems odd but 4 me it's the norm,
Being humble brings you close 2 God,
So I guess I'm pretty far away,
I'm similar to a bomb that's waiting to blow,
How much time remains, at time I don't know,
Let me c what I need 2 c,
Let me be where I need 2 be,
There is only one place 4 me,
That place is simply peace (that's right)

"Distance"

(Dedicated 2 God)

Please 4give me because I know it's been a while,
The two of us haven't spoken but I know I'm still your child.
You've given me rules and at times they were broken,
Through all my ups and downs I clearly heard your words spoken.
I consider small things like the sun peaking through the clouds,
Watching its rays shine upon me as a sweet and simple token.
With so many others in this world it was me that was chosen,
To do your will by using my talents and just when I lose my balance,
You pick me up when I fall, you answer when I call,
Even when the pain is strong you're there through it all.
When it comes to our conversations it's true I miss them,
If you can please 4give me 4 being a bit distant.

"Freedom's Calling"

Leave me alone once I fall asleep,
Please don't wake me until freedom's calling.
I don't care who comes by, just let me rest,
You may only wake me if freedom's calling.

What is that I hear? Is that freedom calling?
I guess not so now I'm stuck awake.
I shall sit in this spot so leave me please,
You may only return if freedom's calling.

What do you want! Has freedom called?
Well if that's not the case why are you here?
Oh I get it, it is crystal clear,
You've been trying to tell me that freedom's here.

But if freedom's here I never heard the call,
The phone is here but it hasn't rang at all,
I understand, the picture is clear for the second time,
Freedom never called because it was always in my mind.

"Healing From Above"

I'm not at ease oh Lord I'm trying,
My pain runs deep but no one sees me crying.
Those who deal the stress don't care about who receives it,
People hear me speak of pain but they don't believe it.
I still could use some help maybe an angel,
Somehow, someway untangle my twisted angles.
Please save me I surrender it all,
Take away whatever you feel must be taken away.
All I want is another chance to serve you Lord,
Just help me because I've lost my way.
You are the truth you are the way and the light,
I've done wrong 4 too long please help me go right.
If you can find a way to have mercy on me,
Only then will the healing begin to take place.

Chapter V: Dedications

"The 11th Day Of September"

Flashbacks come to mind about a certain point in time,
That particular point in time changed everyone's lives.
Without warning planes fell from the sky,
Then crashed into buildings taking innocent lives.
Some people lost husbands and other people lost wives,
Children were killed and we still don't know why.
Was that part of God's plan?
His mercy was shown based on how long those buildings stood.
He held up those buildings as long as he could,
Soon after everything crumbled.
Why did this happen, what was the reason?
The Lord says every storm lasts a season.
That was a day the entire world will remember,
We all still can recall that 11th day of September.

“Life Still Ain’t No Crystal Stair”

(Dedicated 2 Langston Hughes)

Many days, many nights, many tears have fallen,
A lost soul just floats throughout these dark streets,
Who can be trusted, who even cares?
Life is the way it is even though it’s not fair.
Let it be known that life ain’t no crystal stair,
Indeed it’s no crystal stair.

Many weeks, many months, more tears have fallen,
A lost soul just continues to float through life,
A heart made of diamonds now broken into pieces,
Life is the way it is even though it’s not fair,
Let it be known that life ain’t no crystal stair,
Indeed it’s no crystal stair.

"In Loving Memory"

(Dedicated to those we've lost along the way)

In the memory of those who passed before us,
Let us not cry but instead rejoice.
Oh lord, have mercy on the souls that left us,
May their new homes be in your holy house.
If you could please deliver a few words for me,
Maybe these messages will touch the deceased.
Tell Aaliyah that she will always be **One In a Million**,
It's quite obvious she was **More Than A Woman**.
If Lisa ("Left-Eye") can hear me just tell her that,
We shall be smart and not chase **Waterfalls**.
I hope Biggie (Notorious B-I-G) is enjoying his **Life After Death**,
Let it be told that no one is quite **Ready to Die**.
As for 'Pac (2pac), **All Eyez** are still on him,
And **Until the End of Time** we shall search for **Better Dayz**.
Eazy-E you're still remembered, you didn't die in vain,
Without a doubt you're still the realest **Compton City G**.
Tell Pun (Big Pun) that he still is the largest thing,
Because of you players aren't players no more.
Jam Master Jay you'll never be forgotten,
You left us but now you're in God's hands.
So in the memory of those who passed before us,
Let us no cry but instead rejoice.

“Heartfelt Poetry”

(Dedicated to Maya Angelo and Langston Hughes)

Do you know why the caged bird sings?
Can you imagine what a slave used to face daily?
Do you agree when I say life’s no crystal stair?
Those statements and questions all come from poetry,
Who’s poetry am I writing about?
To be honest there are two poets involved.
Maya Angelo and Langston Hughes,
Who are they? They are the reason I write.
My two mentors who inspired my art,
Because of them, I write these words from my heart.

"I'm Sorry"

(Dedicated 2 My Heart)

Allow me to say something I should've said before,
How could I have neglected your feelings?
Throughout my life you've been good to me,
At times you have also been a stranger.
Because of you I often found peace within,
But I can also recall seeing you destroyed.
All I can honesty say is I'm sorry…

You have always been the only true friend I've known,
Because of you so many things were shown,
How I not have protected your feelings?
I guess I was honestly lost.
You are just like me because we're fragile,
How could I have neglected you?
All I can honesty say is I'm sorry.

"Come & Gone"

(Dedicated to Love)

I've been hurt so many times before,
So many tears left my face and dropped to the floor.
I thought they cared, they said all the right things,
But all they wanted was material things.
I know now why the caged bird sings,
It's not fair but life hasn't been and won't be a crystal stair.

So many times my heart has been touched,
They got inside and I instantly cared too much.
What was thought to be love was barely strong like,
I then found myself alone and that's not right.
I know now why the caged bird sings,
It's not fair but life hasn't been and won't be a crystal stair.

"If He Can Do So"

(Dedicated 2 God)

Time and my life years have a lot in common,
They both just keep ticking away.
I've yet to completely find my purpose,
But I get closer to doing so everyday.
Though it may seem pointless I continue to chase,
I continue to chase this thing called love.
But it seems as if I'm chasing the wrong ones,
Which only leads to more tears upon my face.
Time ain't 4ever so each day I ask,
That the good Lord helps me and keeps me safe,
Somewhere between deliverance and erasing my sins,
I hope HE helps me find my ultimate task.

“Cruel Intentions”

(Dedicated to Society)

Is everything exactly what they tell you it is?
Or is everything they tell you what they want you to know?
Who really knows, society shows nothing but lies,
And the government is run by those same crooked lies.
Anyone with a vision that wants to make a change,
Is quickly taken out and the government is to blame.
Abe Lincoln, MLK, Malcolm X, JFK,
Tupac, Christopher Wallace, are only a few names,
How can you fight 4 a nation that doesn’t fight 4 you?
Why be honest with a nation that lies to you?
Why cry when they die, will they cry 4 me?
That’s my reply when they asked if I cried when the Pope died.
Everyday my people die in the streets,
The only thing they received is an all white sheet.
Yellow tape around the scene, little coverage on the news,
Is that fair, is that justified, it’s plain cruel.

"When It's Cold Outside"

(Dedicated 2 Poetry)

You are that one thing that keeps me grounded,
Yet in the same instance you make me feel so high.
When everything is fine or when nothing goes my way,
You give me that ultimate peace.
I love you so much and nothing can change that,
You're always there whenever I need you.
I know I often neglect you but it's not your fault,
Situations come about which alters my thoughts.
If only they could have half a love like this,
The world would truly be a better place.
The truth is I've loved you from the first day we met,
You touched my soul and I connected with you.
You are and will 4ever be my love,
It is you that keeps me warm when it's cold outside.

“A Rose Is Still A Rose”

(Dedicated in memory of Tupac Amaru Shakur)

Today marks the moment twelve years ago,
When a great individual dealt the world a blow,
It hurt me to hear that you died,
Call it what they want to but it’s true I cried.
You made us all express what’s inside,
And told us in many ways that it was cool to cry.
A true rider with ambitions unmatched,
Your emotions were often shown in every one of your tracks.
There were lessons to be learned through your music,
But people were so blind and rarely listened to it.
The only thing those blind people heard,
Were the references to THUGLIFE and multiple curse words.
But there was more to you and they still don’t see,
How a rose can grow right from the concrete.
How a poet speaks, writers write due 2 a spark,
In the eyes of those who follow you, you left a mark.
And that was your intent right from the start,
You’re still that rose that grew from concrete, which touched our hearts.

“MY Heart, My Love…My Mother”

(Dedicated 2 Yolonda Hunter)

You are, have been, and will always be,
The one person who has the biggest affect on me
While most men give flowers and candy to their lovers,
I decided to be different and do something 4 my mother.
Without you I wouldn’t know how 2 treat a women,
To be honest without you I wouldn’t exist.
So on this Valentine’s Day I want you 2 see,
That I love you and without you there wouldn’t be me.
Let this day be different from yesterday and 2morrow,
Enjoy the day because God blessed you with it.
This day is a day filled with love and joy,
And who better 2 give you that than your “baby boy”
Each day spent on this earth should have a purpose,
Everyday on this earth we both go through things.
No matter what I feel or how hard I work,
When I see your smiling face I know my hard work was worth it.
It was I that brought you such wonderful joy,
On that wonderful day of November 23
It would take a lifetime for me 2 pay you back,
So allow me 2 begin by writing you this.
You and I have shared so much and fought many times,
Being a mother unfortunately didn’t come with a manual
But we have both learned and grown over the years,
We’ve made it through the rough times and erased our tears.
If I haven’t said it lately please note this now,
That I love you dearly and each day it grows
With my creative words I hope that love can be shown,
You are my HEART, my LOVE but most importantly my MOTHER.

"Fallen Angel"

(Dedicated to those who can relate)

She was so smart and had lots of promise,
But smart girls weren't too popular.
She wore big glasses and she also had braces,
Girls like that were constantly picked on.
She dressed nice but she was laughed at,
Reason being all of her clothes was not a named brand.
Girls teased her because they were jealous,
Her hair was long and she wore big tails.
Everyday at school her feelings were hurt,
Children made fun of her all day long.
She would try and smile until she went home,
She'd then break down and simply cry.
One day she went to school and the kids made jokes,
But this time her smile seemed different.
She made it through the day and journeyed home,
She grabbed a notepad and wrote this note:
"To those who loved me I'm sorry,
The pain I've endured I'd wish on no one.
I'm sorry that my teeth hide behind braces,
I'm sorry that my clothes are not a named brand.
I can help that my hair is long and pretty,
It's not my fault that my grades are good.
I'm also sorry that I can't carry on,
May God have mercy on those that hurt me.
May God also have mercy upon my soul,
4 I know that my actions will hurt my family.
I never wanted this but I can no longer take this,
Lord 4give me 4 sins 'cus here I come!"
When her parents came home from a long days work,
There were shocked to see the sight that was b4 them.
Their precious daughter who was only 13,
Lay dead on the floor with both wrists slit.
Be advised that your words can affect a life,
Your words are powerful so use them right.

“Fantasy Turned Reality”
(Dedicated 2 Angela P. Robinson)

Every young girl has a fantasy,
Hoping to find that one Prince Charming,
A knight in shinning armor,
Riding a horse and sweeping them off their feet,
Through the way you might catch a glimpse,
But it’s only complete in your sleep,
But 4 you that dream became real,
Somehow it took place when you heard me speak,
From then the journey starts,
A tale of two fragile and recovering hearts,
Through hell and high water,
You and I with God’s help created our daughter,
Though at times I might make you mad,
Hurt your feelings a few times and made you sad,
If you can find it inside,
Deep in your heart and just try,
I’ll try 4 you like I’d die if you,
Were not by my side it’s true that it’s you,
Who can do the things that only you do,
You and your voodoo; you got a hex on me,
And 4 that you get the best of me,
At times you’ve seen the worst of things,
Seen the worst from me, you didn’t deserve to be,
Treated like anything less of a queen,
But u had to accept and see that I’m a king,
That used to be a knight in shinning armor,
Riding in on a horse here to sweep you off your feet,
I’m here to fulfill your dreams,
Let me make a reality out of what you see in your sleep.

"Blessed To Have You"

(Dedicated to my brother, Jeremy Keith Hunter)

I was eight years old when we 1st met,
That's a day I'll never 4get,
I was jealous at 1st I must admit,
But having you around is something I'll never regret,
You and I are as tight as tight can be,
You're the only person close enough to fight with me,
Throw blows with me then I hug my little homie,
I can't stand to be far away from my little homie,
Other than my parents no one really knows me,
But he really knows me I'd die 4 my little homie,
So many late nights we stayed up laughing and playing,
So many late nights you stayed up just praying,
Nobody loves me like you do,
They don't understand me like you do,
I know you look up to me,
Just know that it's you I admire,
Your opinion means the world to me,
And that's because you mean the world to me,
My heart, my conscience at times yes it's you,
Who inspires me to do the very best I can do,
And that's with everything I do,
Before my daughter,
My one inspiration was you!
Words can't express how much I love you,
I thank God 4 blessing me with a brother like you.

"Love @ 1st Sight"

(Dedicated 2 my daughter, Destiny Nevaeh Robinson)

November 5th, 2008 at 6:41 am,
My entire life was transformed,
Transformed into something better,
More mature, a complete metamorphosis,
I've dreamed of this day,
And to finally have it is absolutely great!
To watch you enter into this world,
Is a feeling I've never 4get.
When you first opened up your eyes,
The first thing you saw was me and you smiled,
I've could've cried right there,
It felt so good I could've just died right there,
I had what I always dreamed of,
It was you and you were so beautiful,
So tiny plus you look like your mother,
Mixed with a little of me; you're so precious,
When I first held you in my arms,
I told myself I would not let you near any harm,
As long as I can help it,
You'll be as safe as I can keep you,
Please understand that I c you,
Unlike any other person sees you,
Your mother don't even c you,
The way that I c you and it's with her that I conceived you,
And I can't c you,
The way your mother sees you,
Because you were inside of her,
I always knew I'd be a daddy,
Having you is great it's kind of cool being a daddy,
Just understand you can always come to me,
What's considered new to you ain't new to your daddy,
Probably done seen it and done it before,
Because I was young before,
Even though I'm not a woman,
I understand y'all,
I was raised by one and fell in love with one,
Created you with her and she understands,
Everything you go through because she was young before,
Let it be known I'll destroy anything or anyone,
Who causes you pain even if it's me,
To me you'll always be my baby girl,
My little bundle of joy and I love you,
I love you with all that I am,

And any guy that can't do just ain't no man,
And even if he does he ain't your daddy,
Against me he will lose; nothing beats your daddy,
All I gotta do is c him then size him up,
If I don't like what I c he can't speak to your daddy,
I know what's best 4 you but I'll let you live,
Make your own decisions but please be careful,
What most men they don't even treasure,
And to you it should be priceless,
They wine you dine you,
Lie through their teeth just to get inside of you,
How do I know, no daddy wasn't like that,
But I hung with guys that were like that,
It was ironic to c,
Just how many females like that,
Not to mention a lot of females are like that,
I'll do my best to raise you right so you don't end up like that,
Every time I look in your eyes,
Any stress I might have quickly leaves my mind,
My heart dances whenever you smile,
And my soul hurts badly whenever you cry,
I was asked did I believe love at first is true,
I replied yes indeed I believe that it's true,
I seen the most gorgeous sight in the entire world,
And that was you- Daddy's Little Girl.
I Love U.

"2 My Father"

(Dedicated 2 my father, Eugene Robinson Sr.)

Where do I begin?
How I do start this?
To someone that is to me bigger than life,
A hero in my eyes we even look alike,
Talk the same, walk the same,
We both have the same name,
You always came to my rescue,
No matter how far apart we are,
You always find a way to see me,
Most guys don't even try,
But not you that's why you're not an ordinary guy,
Whenever I need something,
You told me all I had to do was call,
And I feel like I call too much,
But then again I feel like I don't call enough,
Your advice helps me make it through,
You understand how I feel that's 'cus I'm a little you,
Words can't describe what you mean to me,
I know you love me I can feel it in my soul,
You and I rarely say it on the phone,
But we both know it's there,
We both know we care,
When the world ain't fair,
Somehow you manage to make things fair,
Ever since I was a kid,
You never made me feel bad 4 things I did,
That's something I really dig,
I'm gon' incorporate that as I'm raising my kids,
Even though I don't say it much,
Thank 4 you being my dad I love so much.

“Real Talk”

(Dedicated 2 my “pops”, Alvin Keith Hunter)

You took a role ‘cus you loved this woman,
That woman loved you and she had a child,
You treated that child like he was your own,
Played games with him and made him not feel alone,
To him you were like a big brother,
Unaware of the fact that you loved his mother,
In time he grew to love you,
‘cus you loved his mother and it seemed him too,
Through the years we pushed each other 2,
The point of no return but always made it back 2,
Being able 2 speak again,
We spoke as men,
You showed me what I needed 2 know,
Gave me a straight in your face answer,
‘Cus sugar coating does nothing but hold something back,
Sometimes I feel like I haven’t made you proud,
In my mind I hear your words loud,
Thanks 4 helping me not hold my head down,
Even though I don’t say it much I’m glad that you’re around.

“Thank God 4 You”

(Dedicated 2 my grandmother, Cecilia Dooley)

So much love shown,
Treated me like I was your own,
Your house made me comfortable,
It’s like my second home.

If I needed it or wanted it,
You found a way 4 me 2 have it,
Even if my mama said I couldn’t have it,
You’re her mama and *you* said I could have it.

All the dinners you’ve made,
All the nights I spent there and the games that were played,
All the times I came over and always wanted to stay,
All the times you convinced mama to let me stay.

I love you like no other,
I love you even more 4 giving birth to my mother,
I’m grateful 4 you and I love you it’s true,
I thank God 4 giving me a “grinma” like you.

“Always In My Heart”

(Dedicated 2 my Grandparents, Earl and Fannie Robinson)

It’s still hard to come to grips with the fact,
The both of you are gone and ain’t coming back,
Vivid memories of weekend visits,
Getting money from raking the leaves just to run down to Ms. Tyler’s house,
Overload on candy, cakes, chips and pop,
I played ball in the driveway,
My cousins, my daddy, my uncles, or myself,
Spent hours bouncing that ball on the side of the house,
I miss waking up to the smell,
Of granddaddy cooking breakfast,
Grits, eggs, bacon and homemade biscuits,
Syrup and honey right on the table,
Missing grandma outside in the backyard,
Hanging up clothes up on the line,
The only two who had the power,
To keep all the Robinsons in line,
Grandpa after you died,
I felt something snap inside,
I lost my screws when I heard the news,
That you had passed I couldn’t move,
When I walked in the house even though I knew you were gone,
If I walk in the living room I still see you,
I still smell your cigar and see you watching TV,
I just can’t understand why you had to leave,
Grandma you hadn’t seen me in years,
I came home a grown man you almost broke into tears,
You were in the same spot,
Grandpa was in the last time I saw him,
Who knew a few months would pass,
I’d be forced to deal with losing you too,
I know that y’all are gone,
And that’s something I’ll never like,
The one good thing about it is y’all have reunited.
I love you and miss you.

“Unspoken Thoughts”
(Dedicated 2 my Best Friend)

Through the rain,
Through the pain,
We’ve grown so close,
Together we maintained,
You helped me,
I’ve helped you,
We hold each other down,
That’s all we know to do,
You never hesitate,
To tell me when I’m wrong you have never been fake,
Neither have I and that’s just feels,
So good to know at least one person keeps it real,
We support each other,
Even if we don’t agree with it,
We always support each other,
We have a bond like no other,
An unexplainable closeness that’s rarely seen,
The type of closeness mostly seen,
In books, the TV and movie screens,
Through the rain, pain or whatever we went through,
We had each other backs like best friends are supposed to do.

Chapter VI: Final Thoughts

"When the Wheels Stop Turning"

The wheels on the bus go 'round and 'round,
'round and 'round, 'round and 'round.
The wheels on the bus go 'round and 'round,
But one day the wheels will stop.
I can't physically live 4ever but through my works,
My legacy will live until the end of time.
I c death around the corner so I look both ways,
My life will finally end of these days.
And when it's my time I'll kiss the world goodbye,
Then with the Lord I'll reside peacefully up high.
This world was nothing more than pain and stress,
But no matter what I strived to remain the best.
The wheels on the bus may go 'round and 'round,
But one day, one day these wheels will stop.

"A Mission Statement"

(A message from myself to myself)

To truly complete my mission I must,
Become one with my spirit and 4ever elevate.
Trust only those that trusted me,
Love only those that displayed love.
Confide my thoughts in the most sacred places,
Walk softly and speak even softer.
Give the unobtainable, touch the unreachable,
Fly to the most prominent destination,
And sit with an open mind,
Judge not to avoid judgment,
Live to the fullest and consume everything,
Then afterwards die without regret.

www.ingramcontent.com/pod-product-compliance
Ingram Content Group UK Ltd.
Pitfield, Milton Keynes, MK11 3LW, UK
UKHW041431210726
13854UKWH00010B/1657